THIS BOOK BELONGS TO:

I AM PASSIONATE ABOUT:

I AM GRATEFUL FOR:

HAPPINESS IS:

D1133729

Passion, Positivity, Love & Light.

LANCE KITAGAWA

PASSION, POSITIVITY, LOVE & LIGHT.

ISBN-13: 978-0-9975278-0-3
ISBN-10: 0-9975278-0-3

Published by TheHappyProject.com

Book Website
www.thehappyproject.com
Business enquiries and feedback: lance@thehappyproject.com

Printed in the United States of America
First edition, June 2016

DEDICATED TO:

humanity

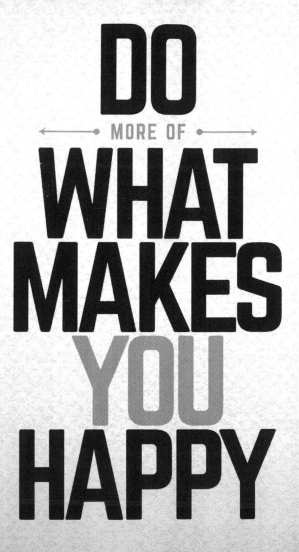

INTRODUCTION

Life is short and no one is promised a tomorrow.
Yet most of us spend our time stressing over things that
are out of our control. Or focusing too much energy on a
job we dislike. Or stuck in a lackluster routine.

Not too long ago I was stuck in such a routine. I had gone
through a divorce. I was struggling at work and yearning
to make more of a difference. In response,
I began creating inspirational images, desperately needing
to be reminded that by doing what I loved and using my
voice, I could have a positive impact on the world.

In this book, I have created daily reminders to inspire you
to live a happier, more fulfilling life. A life full of, among
other things, passion, positivity, love and light. Don't wait
to start living the life of your dreams.

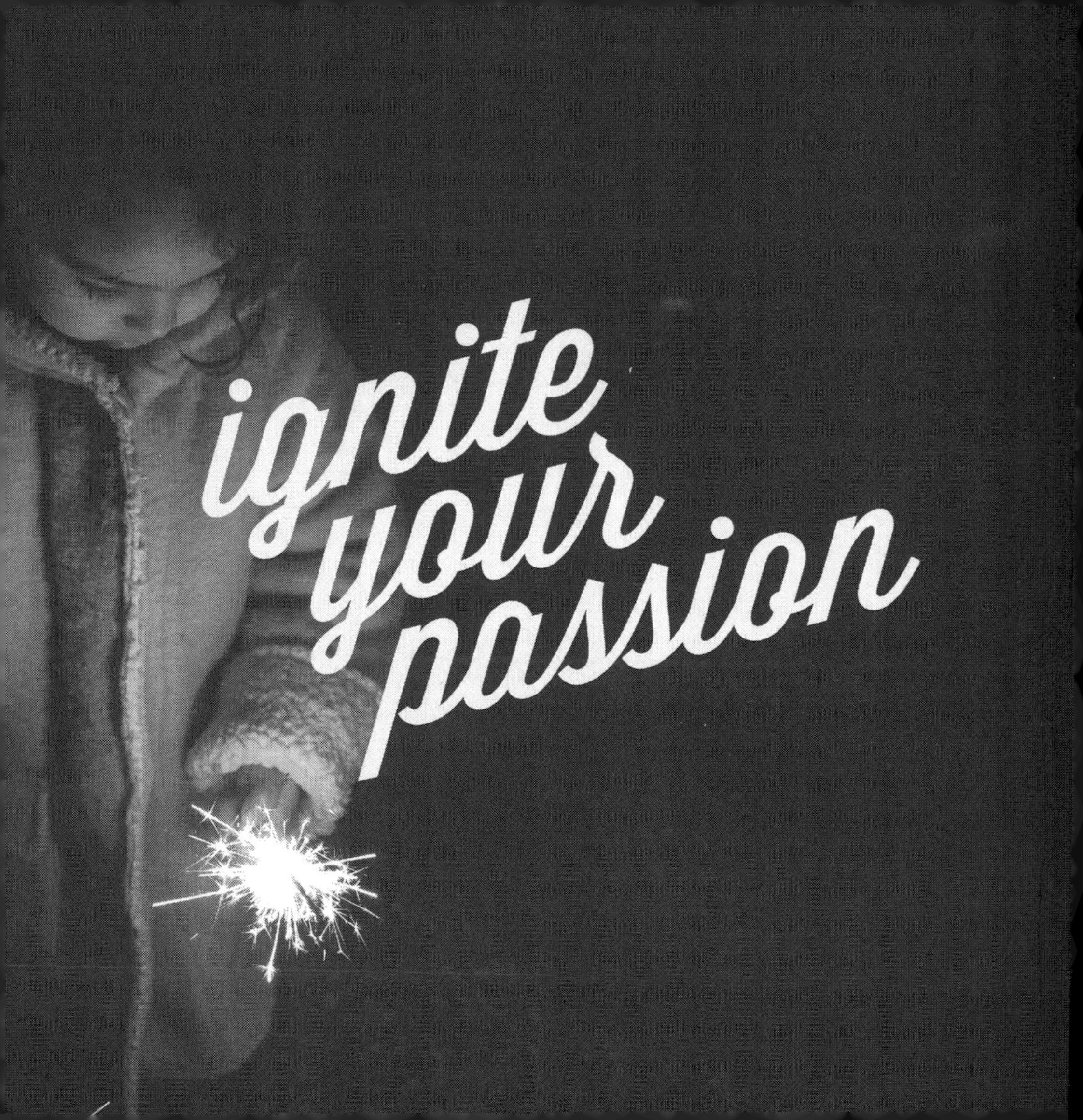
ignite
your
passion

What sets your soul on fire? What ignites your passion? What is your calling? What gives your life purpose and meaning?

Remember to see yourself as a beautiful and significant being, destined to make a difference in the world.

TODAY
is full of
POSSIBLE

How will you leave your mark on the world today?

YOUR UNIQUENESS IS YOUR MAGIC

Your uniqueness is your power. Use your skills and voice to make a difference in a way that only you can. You matter.

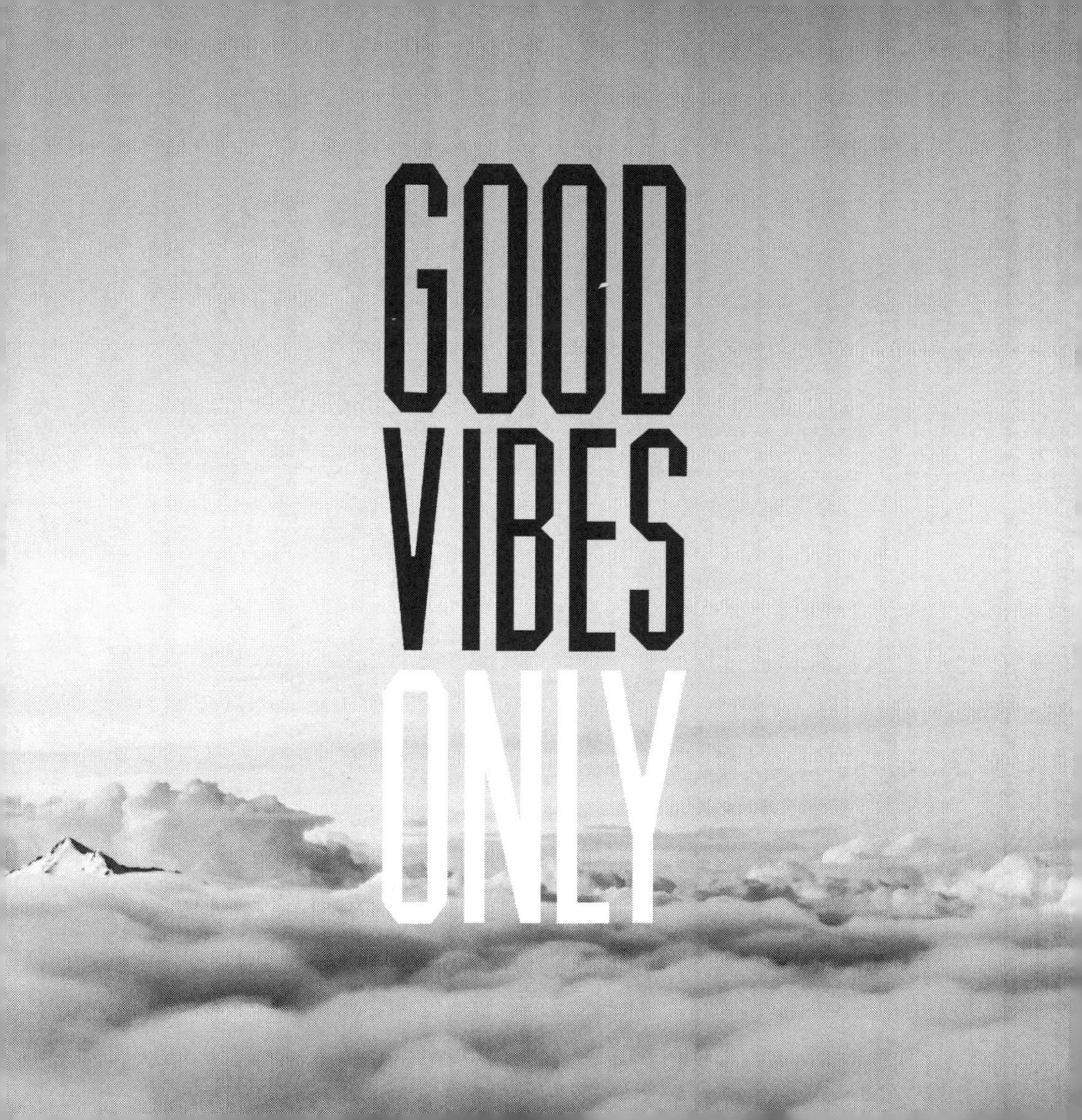
GOOD
VIBES
ONLY

Remember to share your good energy
and positive vibes.

THE GREATEST
WEALTH IS
HEALTH

Remember to take care of your body and mind. Exercise. Eat healthy. De-stress. Be strong mentally and physically…because your greatest source of happiness comes from good health.

SOMETHING GOOD IS COMING

Work hard.

Stay hungry.

Stay focused.

Stay positive.

Know that something good is coming.

first learn how to make *yourself* happy

Figure out what makes you happy and do more of that!

TRUST THE TIMING OF YOUR LIFE

Remember that the universe will bring you what you
need when you are ready. So do what you can to be
ready and trust the timing of your life.

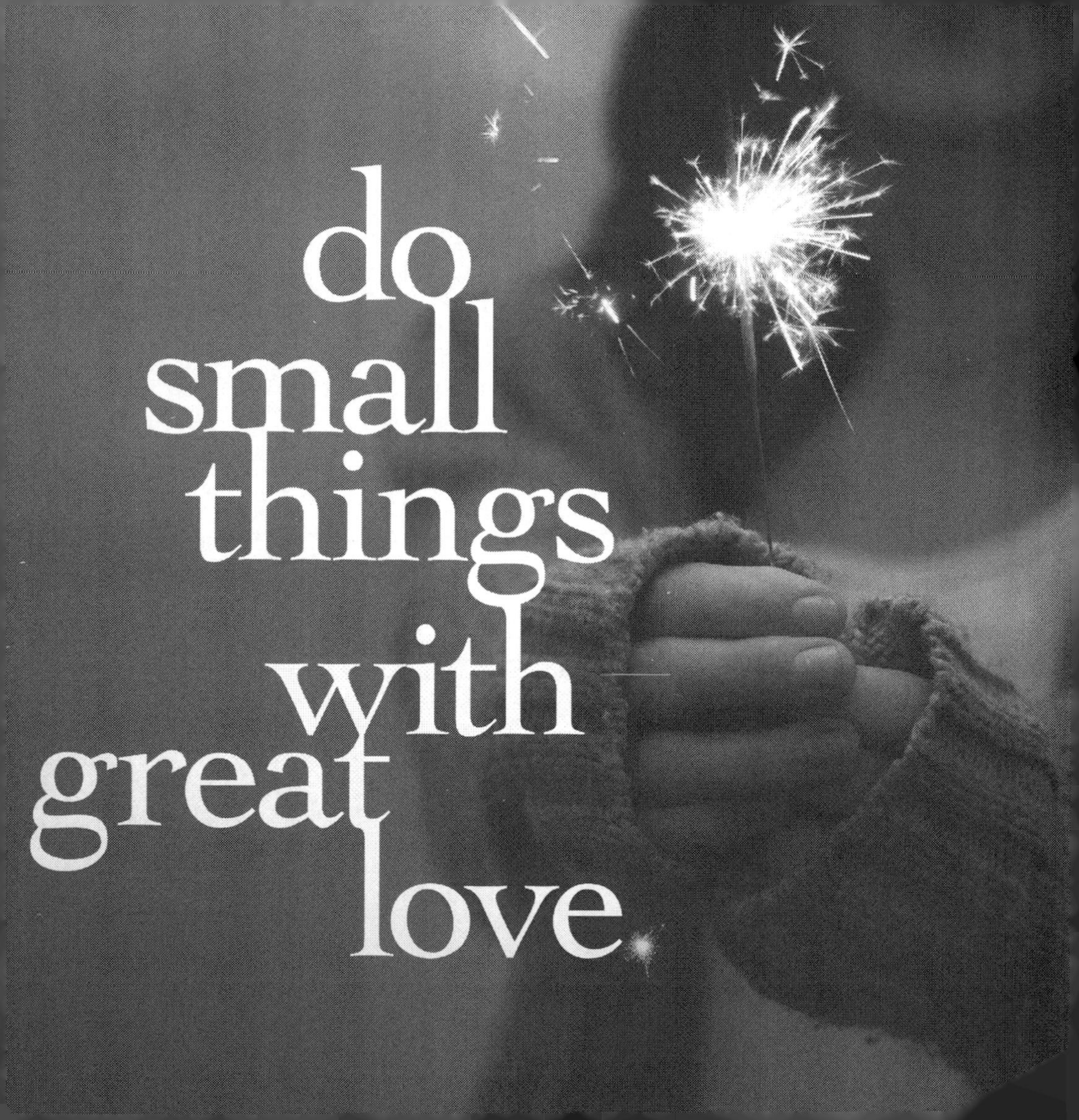
do small things with great love

Do everything out of love and the world will be a better place.

KINDNESS NESS IS FREE

Remember to be generous with your kindness.

Remember to celebrate happiness every day. Surround yourself with positive people. Do what you can to stamp out unhappiness. Do what you love and do what makes you happy.

what's

meant

to be

will

find

a way

Don't worry about anything you can't control. Learn from every experience. Be ready for any opportunity.

make time for
REJUVENATION

Do what makes you feel younger, better and more vital. Make time for relaxing your mind and replenishing your soul.

TELL YOUR STORY

Your story matters. Every bit of it.

SMALL
STEPS
EVERY
DAY

Remember to take the necessary steps, no matter how small, that bring you closer to your dreams.

THE WORLD
NEEDS MORE
PEOPLE WHO
love
THEMSELVES

Loving yourself is not selfish. It is vital and necessary. Find things you love about yourself. Take ownership of your life and know that you are good enough, smart enough and beautiful enough and you are deserving of an abundant life. The world needs you to...show yourself some love!

RISE

SHINE

Remember to pursue your passion. Do what makes you happy. Be your best. Rise and shine today.

YOU'RE GOOD ENOUGH

You have it in you. You're good enough for whatever life you want for yourself. Remember that and make it happen…

ASPIRE

TO

INSPIRE

BEFORE YOU

EXPIRE

Inspire.
Uplift.
Motivate.
Help.
Encourage.

LET'S BE

BETTER

HUMANS

The Earth needs us to be better humans.
Animals need us to be better humans.
Humans need us to be better humans.

BE UNSTOPPABLE

Find your passion, make it your purpose and
be unstoppable.

What are you thankful for?

SURROUND YOURSELF
WITH PEOPLE
WHO REMIND YOU
OF THE FUTURE,
NOT THE PAST.

Remember to surround yourself with people who lift you up and inspire you to strive for a better future.

ANOTHER
SUNRISE
ANOTHER
CHANCE

Each new day brings hope and a chance to grow,
a chance to improve your life and a chance to get
closer to realizing your dreams.

PEOPLE LOVE YOU BECAUSE YOU'RE YOU

Don't try and be anyone else. Don't compare yourself to others. You are loved because of who you are.
Just be you.

#dreambig

Dream big and be brave enough to passionately pursue your dreams.

you matter

Every human being has value and has something to contribute to this world. Remember that you matter!

Enjoy every moment, appreciate the people you meet along the way and learn from every experience. This is your journey. Make it memorable.

this

is your

journey

Manifest
Your
Dreams

Believe in yourself, let go of all fears and
visualize what you want your life to be.
Don't be afraid to manifest your dreams.

put a smile, on someone's face

Make someone smile. Make someone laugh.
Make someone so happy that their face lights up.

BE WHO YOU
WANT TO BE

Be awesome.
Be beautiful.
Be you.

YOUR LIFE
IS YOUR MESSAGE
TO THE WORLD

Find your purpose, follow your passion, create with your unique voice and do what makes you happy.

Remember that your life is your message to the world. So make it memorable. Make it meaningful. Make it happy.

LIFE IS ABOUT CREATING YOURSELF

Remember to create your best self and create a life you truly desire.

DO WHAT MAKES YOU HAPPY

What makes you happy? What gives you joy and makes you feel at peace? Figure out what makes you happy and do more of those activities. Be grateful. Cross something off your to-do list. Pursue your passion and find your purpose. Spend more time with the people you love.

MAKE WHAT YOU DO
MATTER

Love what you do.
Find purpose and meaning in what you do.
Make what you do matter.

reach great heights

Stay focused and committed to your purpose and passions and you will reach great heights.

NO BEAUTY SHINES BRIGHTER THAN THAT OF A GOOD HEART.

The most beautiful people in the world are those
with the biggest hearts.

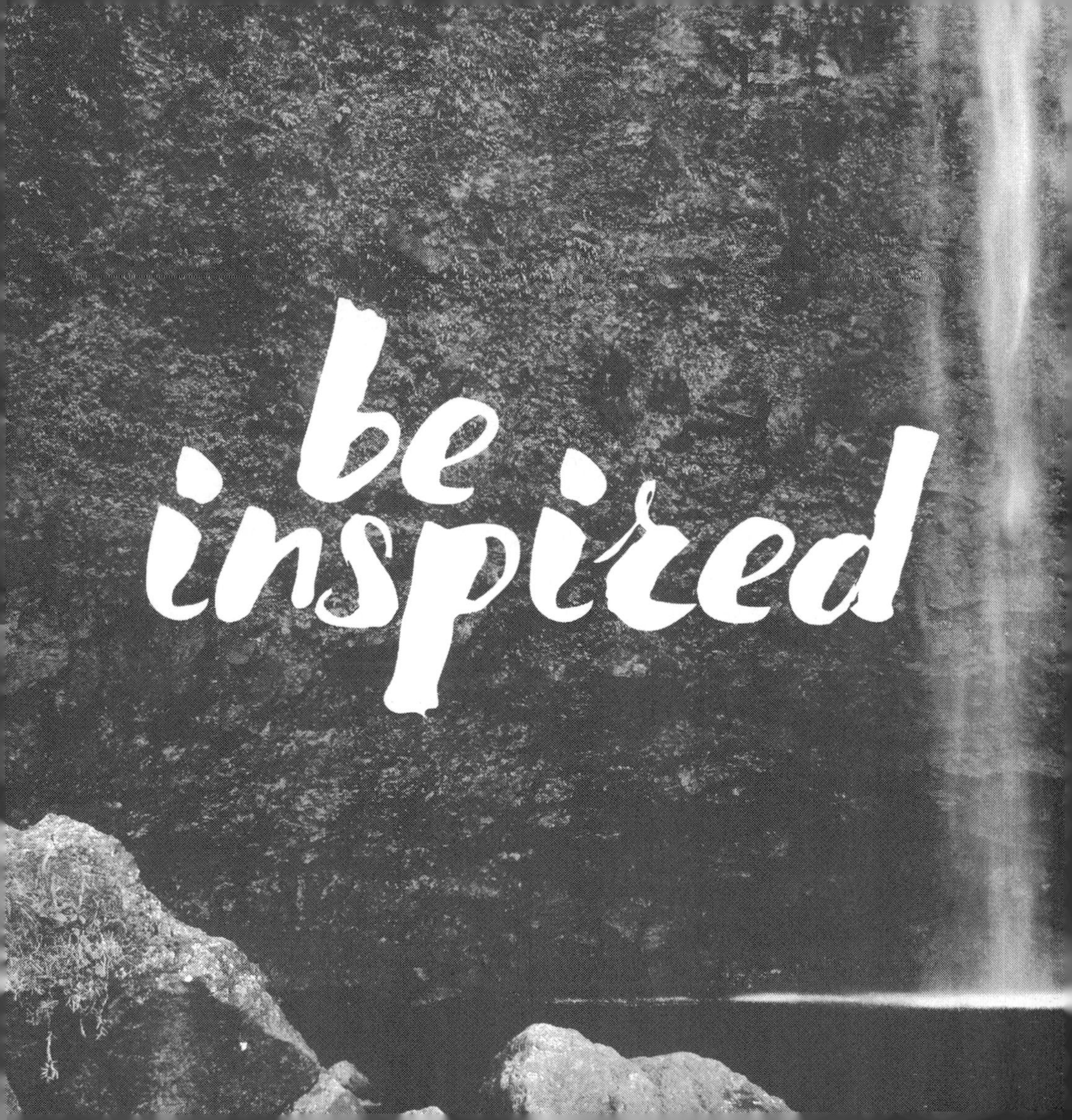
be
inspired

Inspiration is everywhere.
Be inspired and inspire others.

Blossom where you
are planted

Instead of complaining and making excuses,
remember to always make the best of your situation.
Bloom where you are planted.

My primary mission for this project is to touch someone's heart. I have always enjoyed inspiring others but it was in college that I realized I had the power to touch someone's heart through design... and I have been yearning to do so ever since. Opportunities have come and I have worked on some rewarding campaigns for foundations and charities. Now I want to devote my life to touching peoples' hearts...

HONOR YOUR CALLING

Remember that if you are breathing, you have an important contribution to make to this world. If you truly want to come alive…find the reason you were born. Find your calling and honor it.

take nothing for granted

Imagine living without clean water. Without a home. Without food. Or without your health. Appreciate what you have. Take nothing for granted.

THERE IS NO BETTER DAY THAN TODAY TO START LIVING YOUR DREAMS

Live the life that you want to live. Make changes to improve the quality of your life. Find your purpose. Go after your dreams!

live simply

Remember to fill your life with simple joys and be grateful for each and every moment.

OWN
WHO
YOU
ARE

Fall in love with everything that makes you...

...you.

inspire possibility

I love the feeling of empowering people to be
who they truly are. Helping them embrace their
individuality and come alive. And motivating people
to go after their dreams and find their purpose.

Remember to surround yourself with awesome peeps
and inspire possibility!

I CAN
I WILL

Remember that you can do anything you set your mind to. Pursue your passions with dedication, purpose and focus, and you can achieve greatness.

If you heal yourself first, you can more effectively heal others. The more you are able to love and respect yourself, the more you can love and respect others.

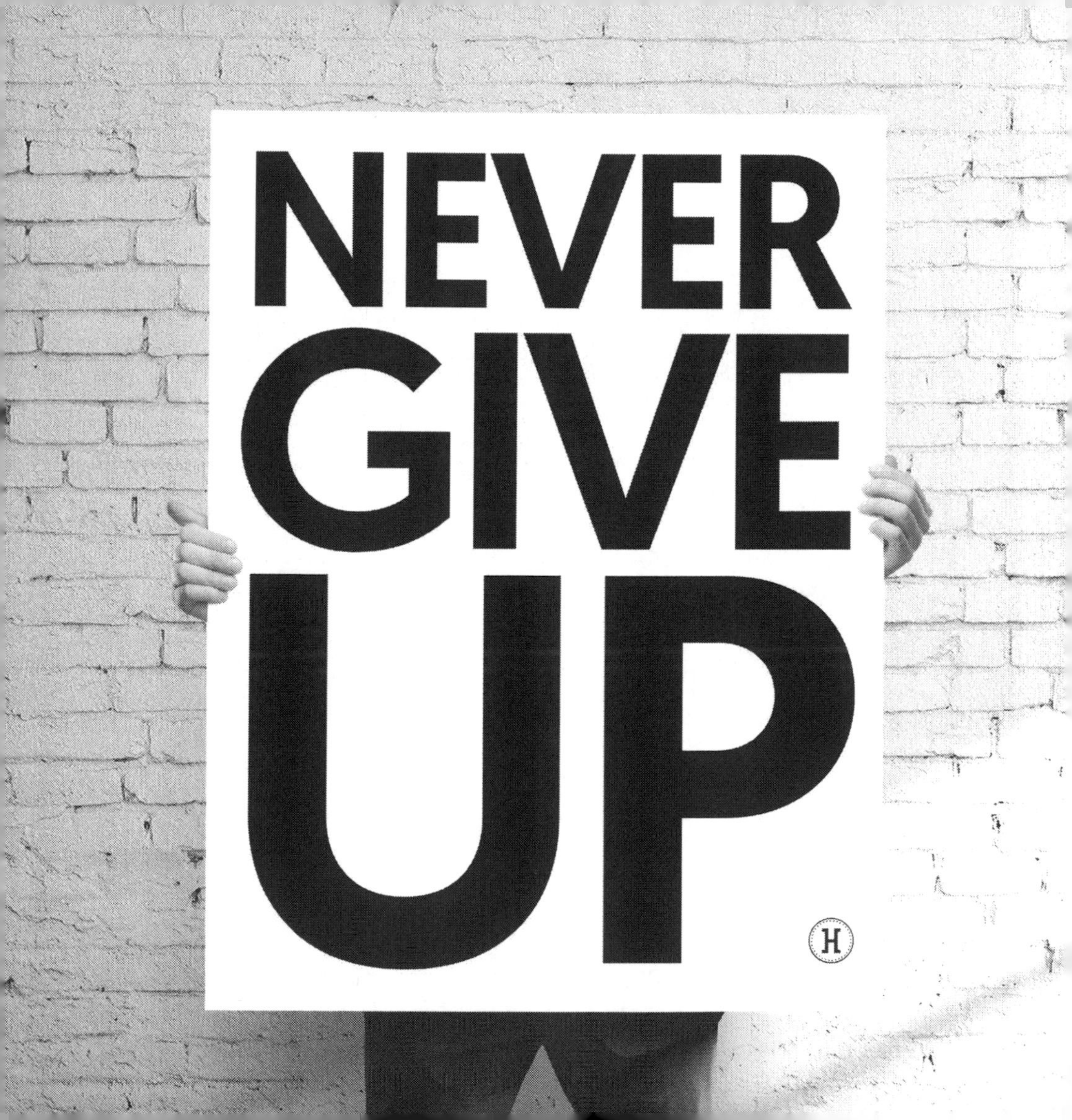
NEVER
GIVE
UP

You are loved.

open your mind.
feed your soul.

Open your mind to new uplifting experiences.
Let your passions ignite your soul. Find your place
of peace and happiness.

CREATE
THE
THINGS
YOU
WISH
EXISTED

Create something amazing.
Create something you want to see in the world.

STAY
MOTIVATED

Health is a vital piece of your happiness.
Set goals to keep your mind and body healthy.
Stay motivated to achieve them.

BE
FEARLESS

Don't let fear hold you back from doing what your heart wants to do, and being who you are truly meant to be.

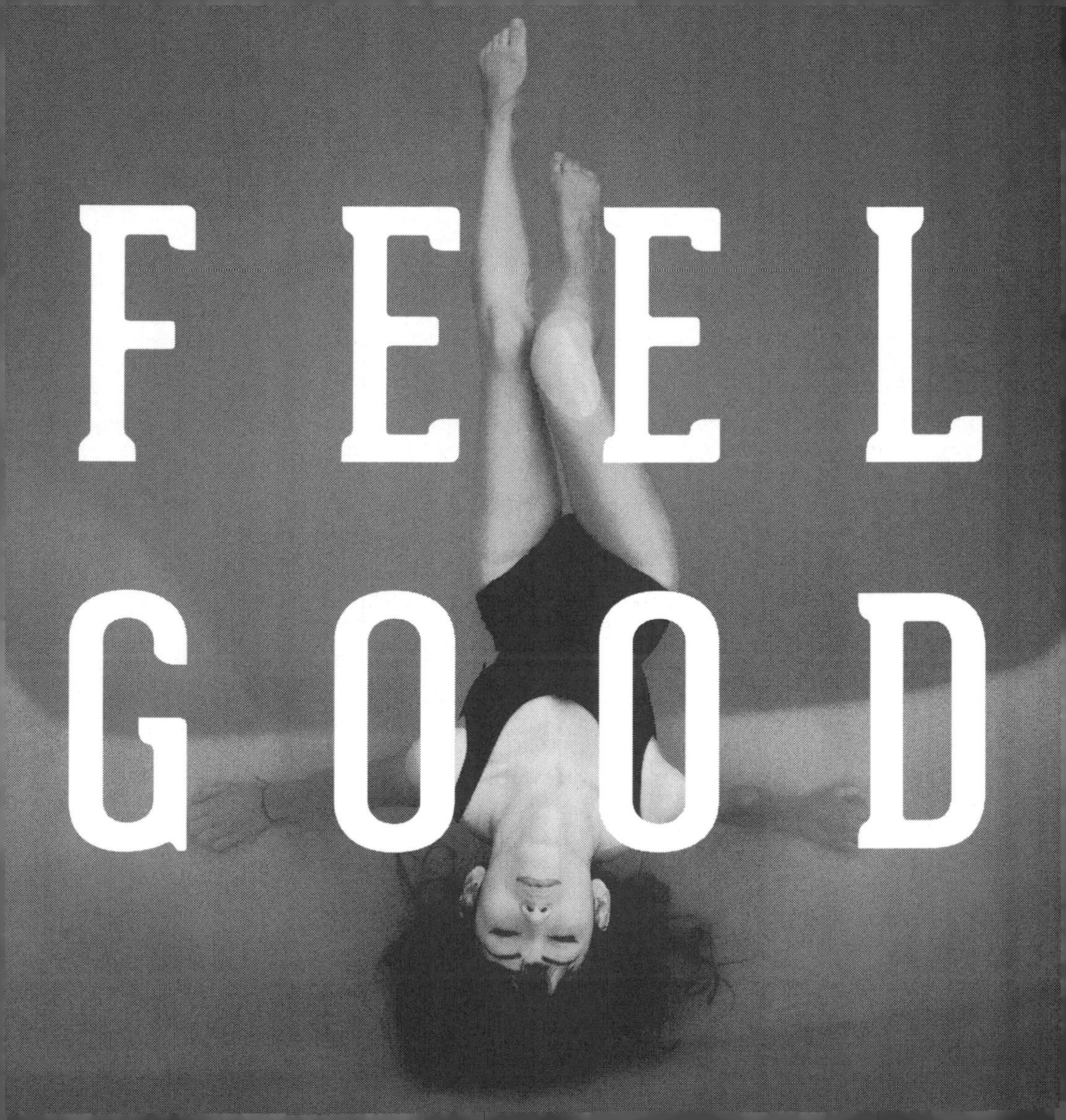
FEEL
GOOD

Remember to do what makes you happy.
Do what you love.
Do what makes you feel good.

THERE'S ALWAYS ROOM TO BE A BETTER YOU

Remember to grow every day.

Learn something new.

Improve your life.

Love more.

Be more positive.

Be more patient.

Be more passionate.

Be more grateful.

Be more tolerant.

Respect all living beings.

Take care of our planet.

Take nothing for granted.

Be an ambassador of good.

Practice more kindness.

Make healthier choices.

Eat better and drink more water.

Nurture your body and soul.

Make happiness a priority.

DO SOMETHING EVERY DAY THAT MAKES YOU HAPPY

Think about all of the things and activities that make you happy and do one of those every day. You will be happier doing the things you love and you will be more grateful for everything on your list.

SIMPLIFY

Simplifying your life will lead to more peace, more time for gratitude and more time to spend on your passions.

THE GRASS
IS ALWAYS
GREENER
WHERE YOU
WATER IT

Focus on what makes you happy, brings you joy
and ignites your passion.

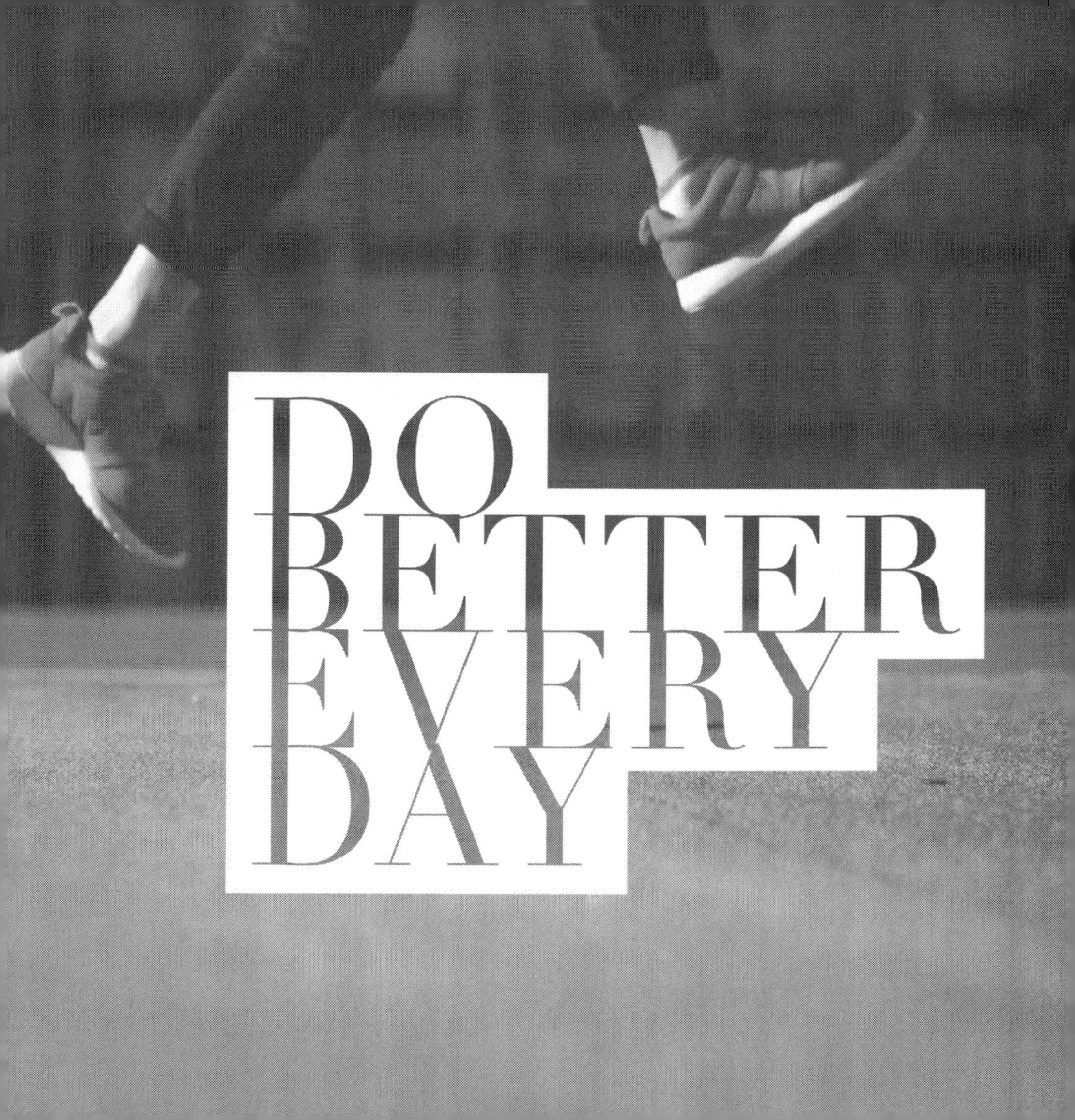
DO
BETTER
EVERY
DAY

Remember to challenge yourself to be a better person every day.

embrace *the.* morning

Wake up and realize you are blessed with a new day. Start the day with gratitude and positive thoughts and carry that through with purpose and productivity. Do what makes you happy today.

ALIVE & BLESSED

Some days are harder than others and we need a reminder to latch on to something positive, count our blessings and find beauty in that day.

find·inner peace

Live honestly.
Always do the right thing.
Find your place of peace.

HAPPINESS
CAN BE FOUND
ANYWHERE

Make a conscious choice to be happy and be grateful for what you have.

FALL IN LOVE WITH YOUR LIFE

Remember to fall in love with your life...every minute of it.

let your heart

SOAR

Let love be your guide as your heart and soul rises to the greatest of heights.

Happiness is living a life of purpose.

WHAT'S YOUR WHY?

Your 'WHY' is so important. It's your purpose. It's the reason for doing what you do. It's what gives meaning to your life and gets you out of bed in the morning.

So what's your 'WHY'?

FILL YOUR SOUL

Remember to fill your soul with gratitude, passion, love
and anything that inspires you and makes you happy.

FIND YOUR CALLING

Remember to follow your heart. Pursue your passion.
Find your purpose. Create a meaningful life.

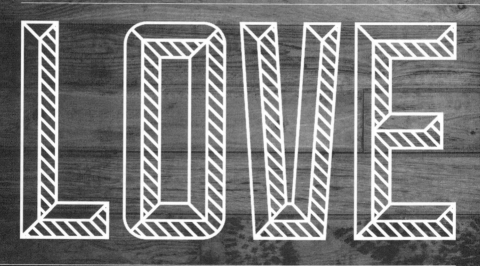

DO WHAT YOU

LOVE

WHAT YOU DO

Happiness is doing what you love and loving what you do.

perfect your
CRAFT

Hone in on your passion.
Dedicate your life to your purpose.
Perfect your craft.

A smile is the universal language of kindness and a beautiful expression of happiness. Remember to smile wherever you go.

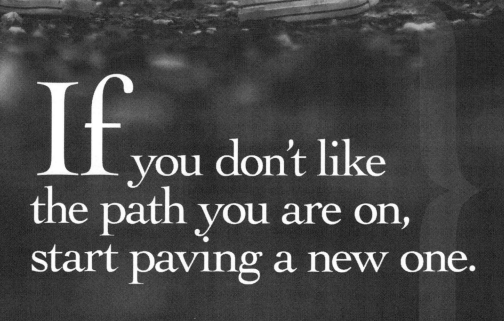

If you don't like the path you are on, start paving a new one.

If you don't like your current situation, start making changes. Create a life you love.

HAVE AN ATTITUDE OF GRATITUDE

Be grateful for everything you have in your life right now. There are many who have much less. Thank the people and experiences that have helped you get to where you are. Appreciate the small things.

BY ALL MEANS, KEEP MOVING.

Remember to keep hustling. Keep learning.
Keep growing. Keep following your passion.
Keep going after your dreams. Keep doing
what you love. Just keep moving.

STAY HUNGRY
STAY FOOLISH

Be humble and grateful.
Push yourself to be better every day and also
daring enough to change the world.

★

LIVE LIKE THERE IS NO TOMORROW

★

Do what makes you happy today.
Tell someone you love them today.
Spread kindness today.
Build your dream today…

PUSH YOUR LIMITS

Just a little reminder to push yourself to be the best
that you can be!

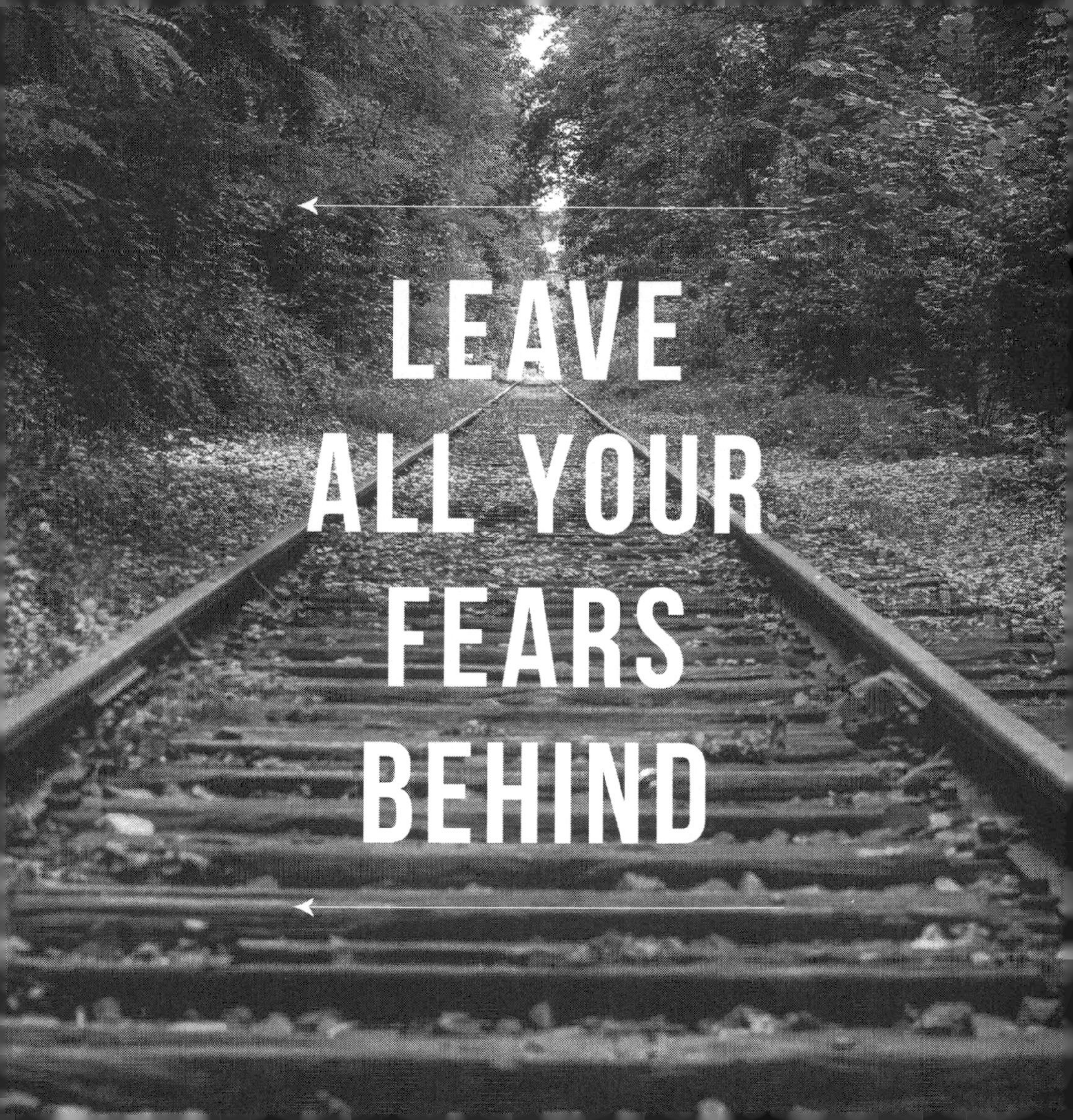
LEAVE
ALL YOUR
FEARS
BEHIND

Don't let fear keep you from achieving your dreams.
Overcome all obstacles. Deflect all negativity.
Slay all demons. Leave all your fears behind.

Get out and explore nature.
Surround yourself with wonder.
Take in a beautiful view.

MAKE ★ IT ★ HAPPEN

Some people want it to happen, some wish it would happen, others make it happen.

Create a life you love. Follow your passion and do what makes you happy. Be someone who makes it happen.

Clear your mind of stress and dwell on whatever
brings more joy into your life.

HONOR YOUR SELF

Remember that honoring yourself, respecting yourself and falling in love with yourself...are keys to your happiness.

LOVE
is
LIFE

Spread love today.

TOMORROW
YOU WILL
WISH YOU
HAD STARTED
TODAY

Follow your dreams and your passions. Do what you love and makes you happy. Start making changes TODAY…

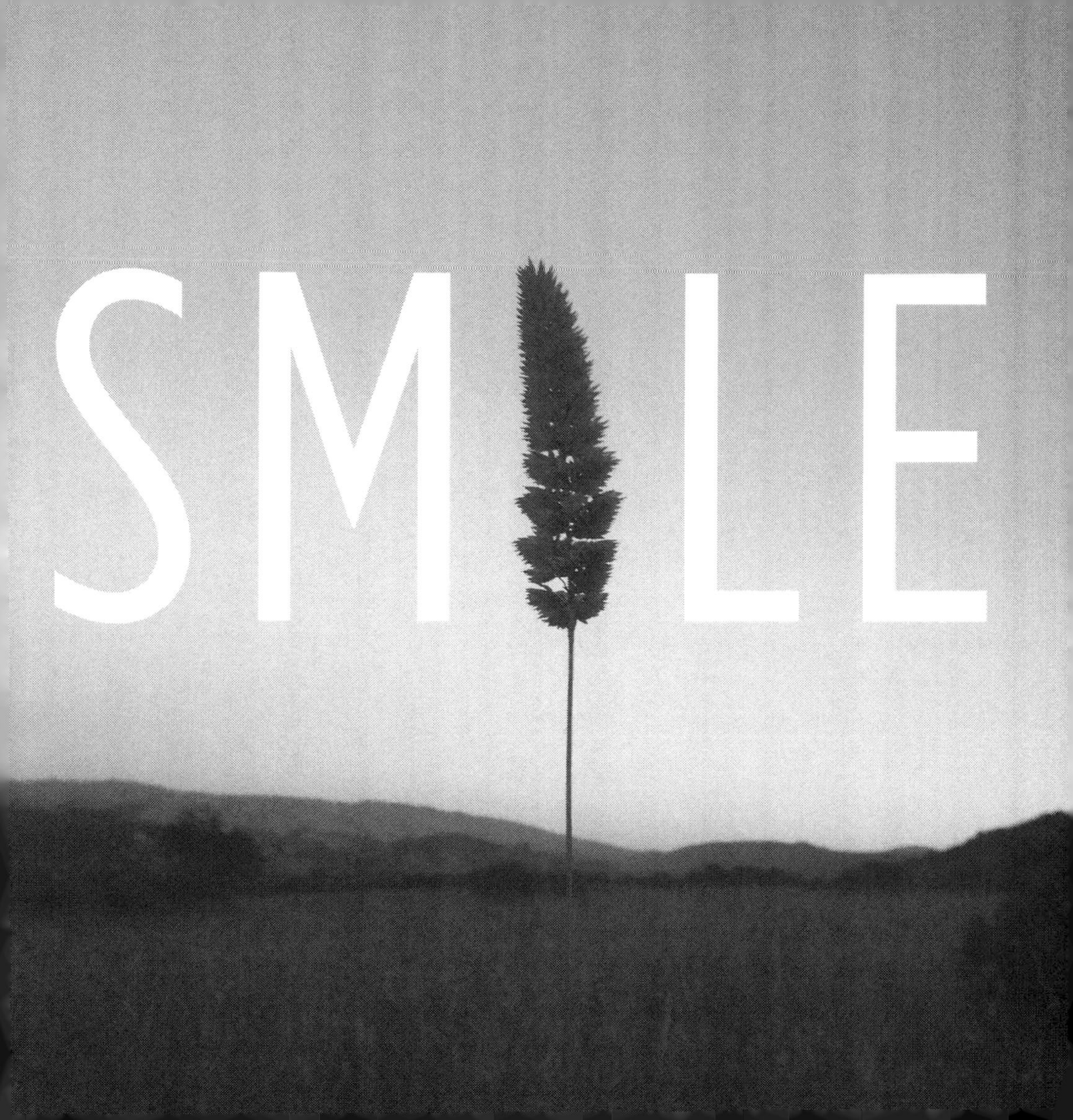
SMILE

Radiate positivity. Spread hope and happiness.
Pay it forward. Touch someone's heart. Smile.

LIVE IN HARMONY

Live with love and respect, acceptance and tolerance,
kindness and gratitude. Live in harmony with
yourself and the world around you.

YOU DECIDE
WHAT KIND
OF DAY IT IS

Find the good in each day.
Do what you love.
Find beauty in each day.
Do what makes you happy.

you're the author
of your own
life

This is your life. Your story.
What will you write today?

WE'RE
all
IN THIS
TOGETHER

A shout out to the people who lead, teach, inspire and uplift. Keep spreading positivity and changing the world. All humans deserve love and happiness.

move
your
life
forward

Remember to keep moving forward. Take that next step. Be brave and take risks. It's not about how fast you are going. It's about progressing every day, learning from your experiences and getting closer to realizing your dreams.

DON'T STOP
UNTIL YOU'RE
PROUD

Keep going until you're proud of yourself and everything you have accomplished. Don't give up. You'll get there.

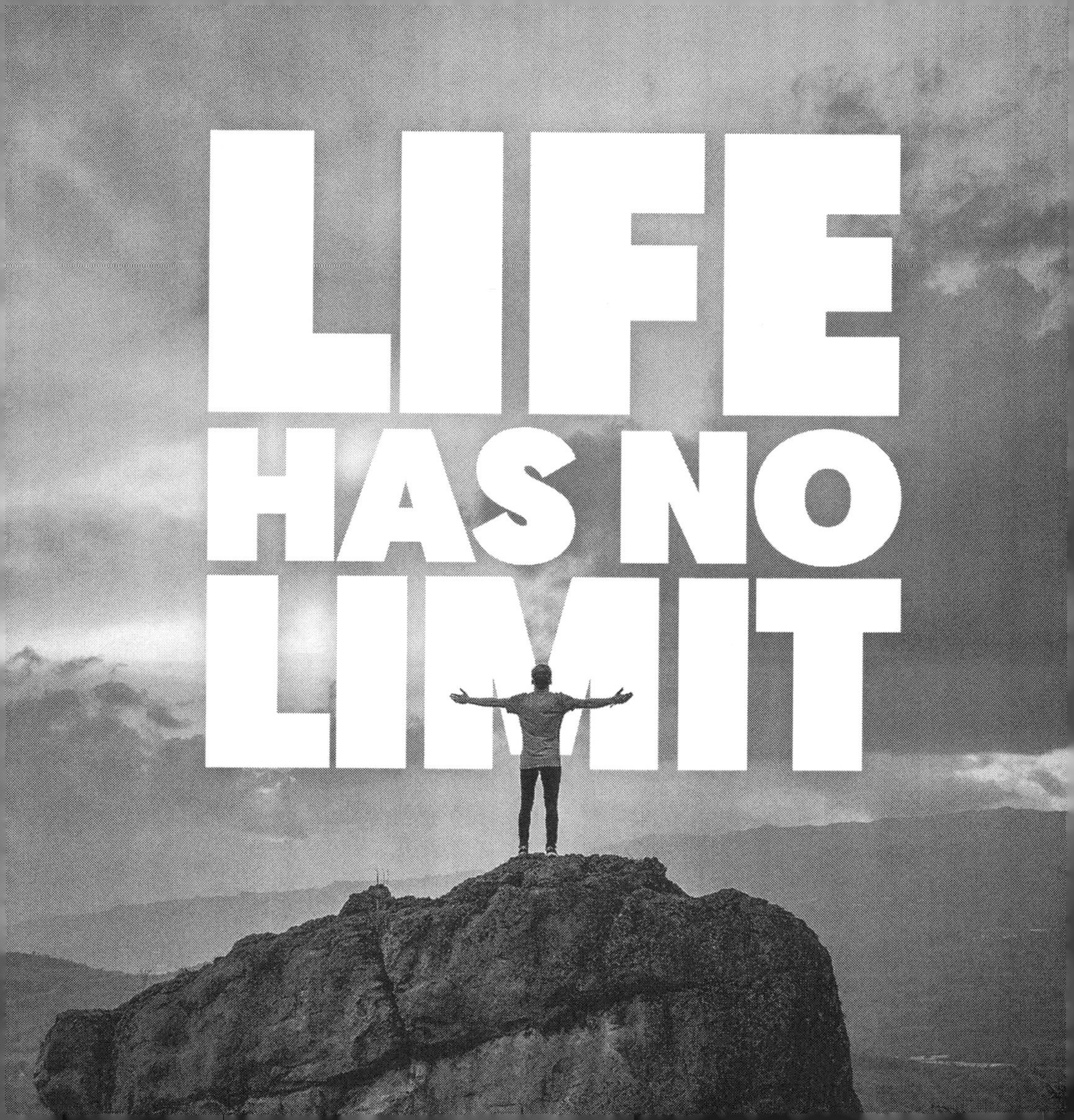
LIFE
HAS NO
LIMIT

There's no limit to what you can accomplish.
Know that you are capable and deserving.
Pursue your dreams.

STAY POSITIVE
NO MATTER WHAT

No matter what life throws at you...stay positive.

be a blessing

Remember to be a blessing to someone today.

share your
AWE
SOME
NESS
with the world

YOU ARE AWESOME!

Remember that...

GET
$#%!
DONE

Be productive. Cross off those pesky little tasks on your to-do list. You'll have more peace of mind and more time to think about and do what makes you happy.

A DIFFICULT ROAD CAN LEAD TO A BEAUTIFUL DESTINATION

Keep going. Don't give up. Remember that it is often the hardest roads that lead to the most beautiful places.

REMEMBER
WHY
YOU
STARTED

I started creating these images because I wanted to put some positivity out into the world. I wanted to inspire and help people. And I want to live a life that I absolutely love.

What's your WHY?

DON'T WAIT FOR OPPORTUNITY.
CREATE IT.

Create your own opportunities.

HAPPINESS IS A GOOD BOOK

What's the most memorable book you've read?
What book has changed your life?

START TODAY

Follow your heart.

Make a change.

Do what makes you happy.

Find your passion.

Get an exercise routine going.

Give your life purpose and meaning.

Start today.

FIND YOUR BEST SELF

AND HOLD ONTO IT FOR DEAR LIFE

Find your purpose in life.
Find your passion.
Find what fuels your happiness.
Find your best self.

[LIVE IN THE
MOMENT]

We aren't promised tomorrow so make the most of today!

KEEP THE EARTH HEALTHY

Never forget that the earth doesn't belong to us. Wherever you go…leave that place better than when you found it. Same with the people and animals you interact with…treat them all with respect and pay your kindness forward.

LOVE
the
LIFE
you
LIVE

We only get one life. Love your life. Be grateful. And if there is anything in your life that you are not happy with...make some changes.

Remember to be kind to everyone you meet.

LIVE LIKE THERE'S NO TOMORROW

The present is a gift we are all blessed with.
Be grateful. Do what makes you happy today.

consistency is key

Being consistent and genuine will play a huge part
of your success.

NEVER LOSE YOUR SENSE OF
WONDER

Remember to enjoy the beauty that surrounds you and appreciate the wonders of nature. Constantly seek new experiences and new adventures.

NO WHINING

NO COMPLAINTS

NO EXCUSES

Life is short…it's not worth spending your time making excuses and complaining. Make a change if there is something negative in your life.

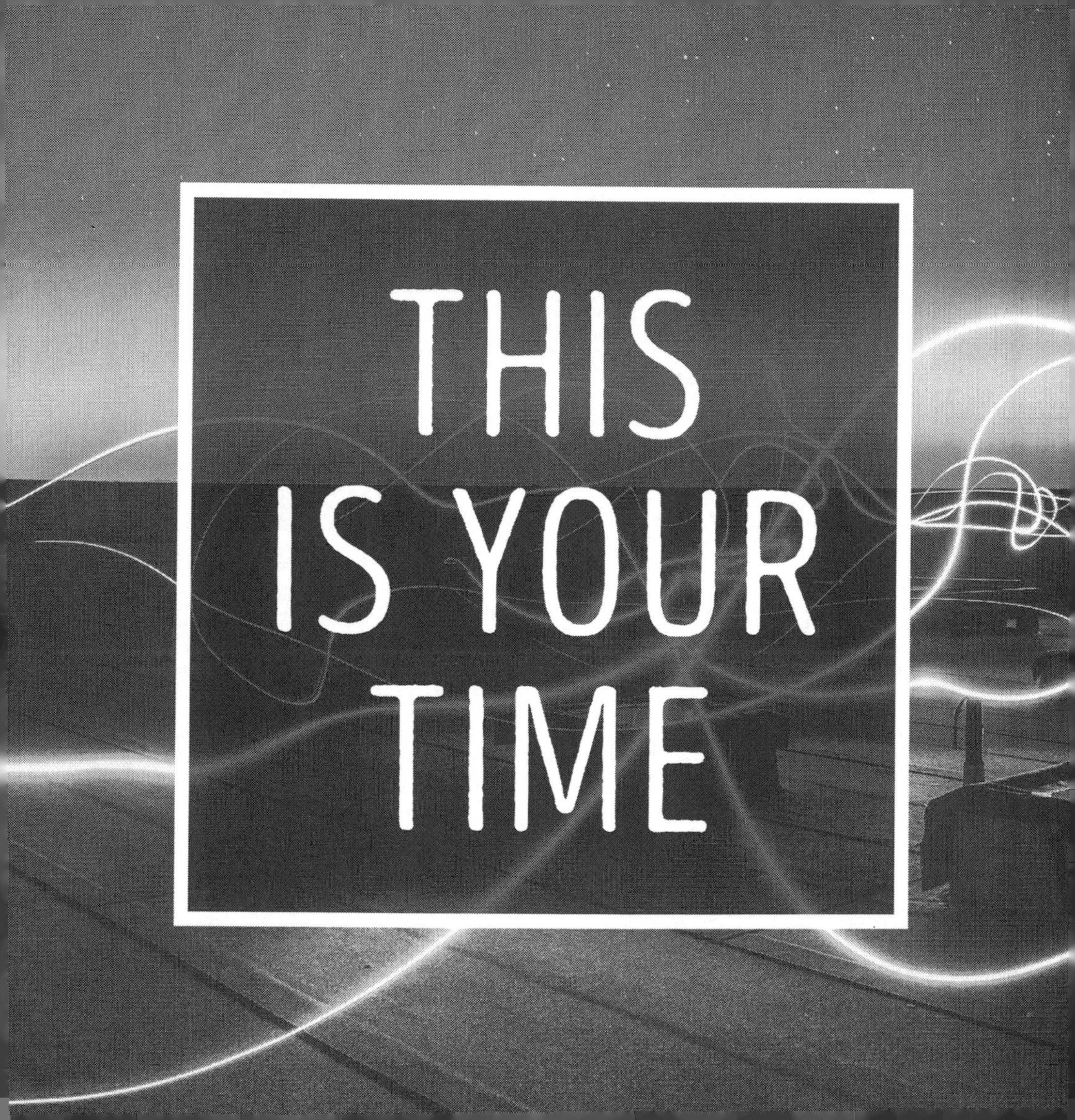
THIS
IS YOUR
TIME

Follow your passion, find your purpose and do what makes you happy. This is your time.

Remember to take the time to relax your mind, body and spirit.

be
the
change

Let's change the world.

Give kindness.
Give compassion.
Give love.

Do good and good will come to you.

DREAM MORE.
DO MORE.
BECOME MORE.

Strive to become more.

Yearn to inspire more.

Aim to love more.

NEVER LOSE YOUR SENSE
of WONDER

Be in awe of the beauty that surrounds you.
Stay hungry. Be grateful. Explore the world
with a sense of wonder.

INSPIRATION IS EVERYWHERE

Be inspired.

» ALLOW YOUR

PASSION

TO BECOME YOUR

PURPOSE »

My passion is inspiring people to live a happier life.
My passion has become my purpose.

What's your passion?

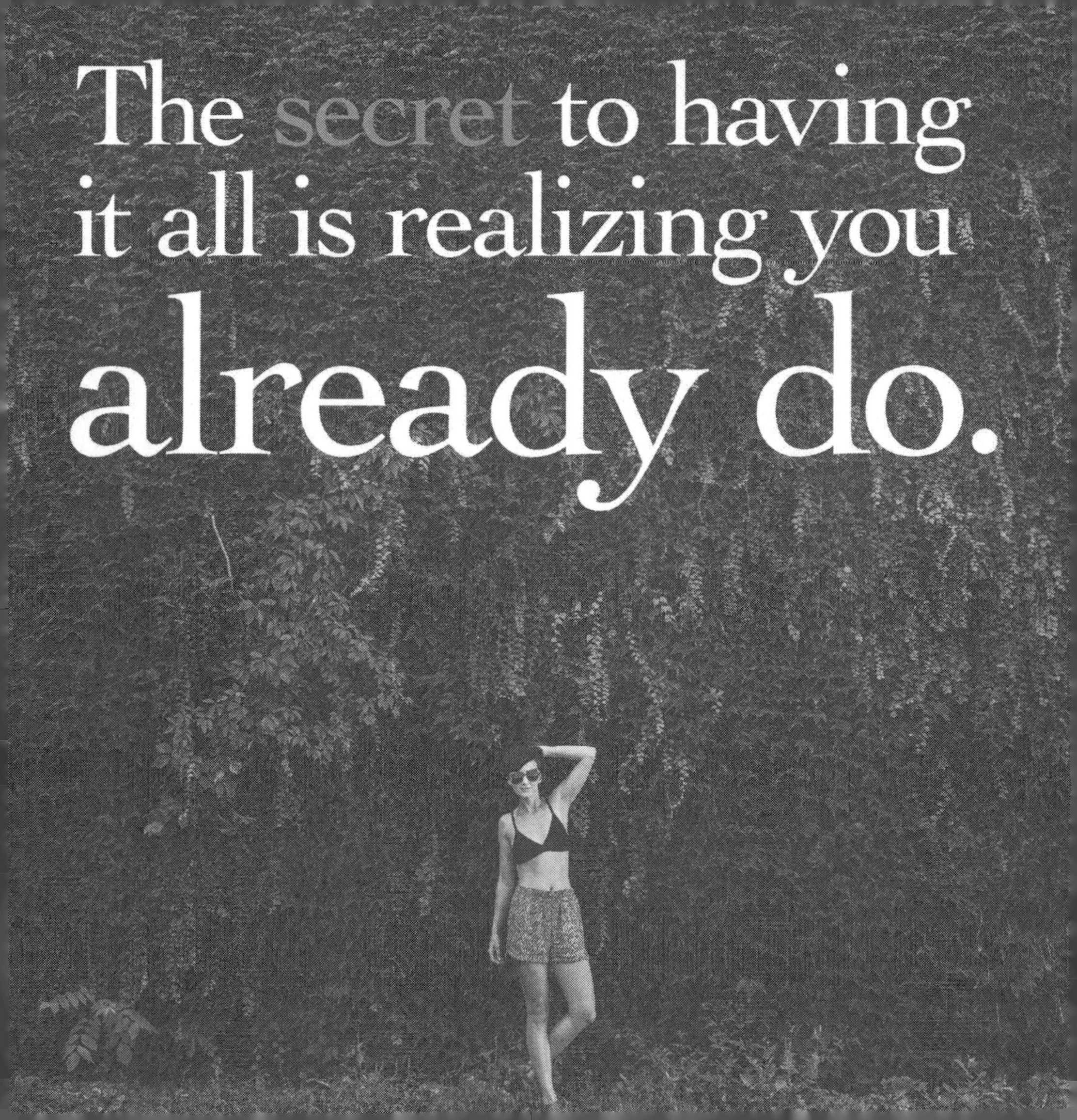
The secret to having
it all is realizing you
already do.

Remember to appreciate what you have.

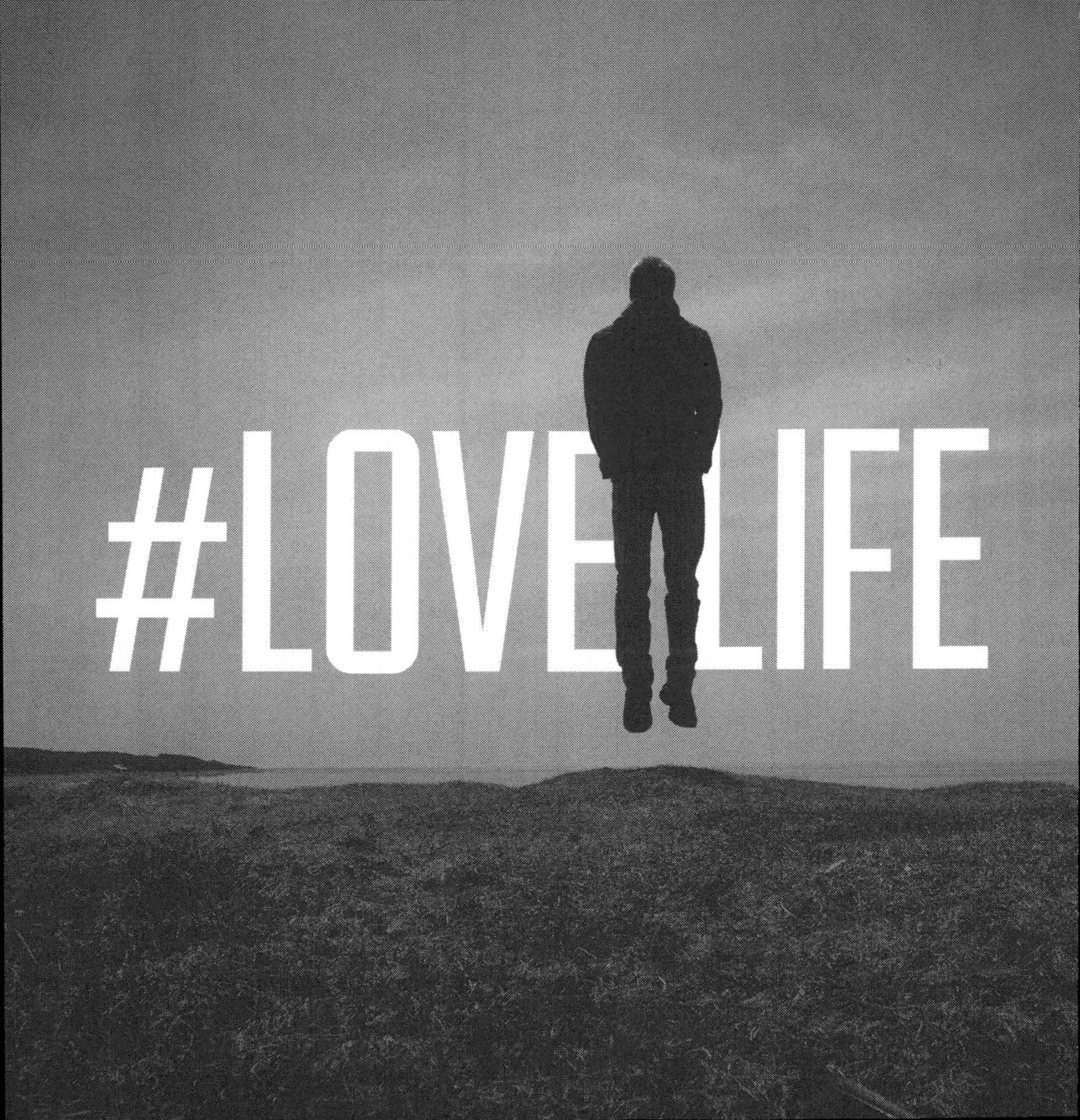
#LOVELIFE

Remember to love your life and spread love
wherever you go.

follow your

BLISS

Trust your heart and follow your bliss.

[BE IN THE PRESENT]

Remember to treat each and every moment as a gift. Allow yourself to be present and come alive in those moments.

APPRECIATE

the little things

THAT MAKE LIFE GREAT

Don't forget about the little things. They often become big things or lead to something greater.

Do good.
Spread love and kindness.
Make the world a better place.

oh so grateful

Remember that there are people who would be more than happy with what you have.

IT'S A
SWEET
SWEET
WORLD

We live in an amazing world. Appreciate it.
Take care of it. Strive to make it even better...

SOMEWHERE SOMEONE HAS IT MUCH WORSE THAN YOU

Remember to be grateful, work hard and be kind…
and amazing things will happen.

MAKE THE MOST OF THE TIME YOU ARE GIVEN

We are given precious little time on this planet. Find your passion and purpose in life. Do what you love and do what makes you happy. Make the most of your life.

Life isn't about waiting for the storm to pass…It's about learning to dance in the rain. Don't waste your time waiting for the right moment. Remember to live your life in the present, do what makes you happy and enjoy the journey.

Life is precious.
Every day is a gift.

find your passion

Find your passion. Do what makes you happy.

DON'T
STRESS OVER
SOMETHING
YOU CAN'T
CHANGE

Focus on the things you can change instead of stressing over anything beyond your control.

ADVENTURE AWAITS

Go on adventures. Seek new experiences.
Make more memories. Explore different perspectives.
This beautiful world awaits.

find **joy** *in the* *journey*

Find joy in your day.
Enjoy the little things.
Enjoy the journey.

YOU
WIN
OR
YOU
LEARN

From every experience you either win...or you learn,
progress, change and grow.

ALWAYS LOOK ON THE
BRIGHT
SIDE

Not every day will be good, but it's important
to find the good in every day.

enjoy today

Make the most of today.

Don't take life too seriously.

STAY TRUE
to
YOU

Celebrate your unique qualities, your perspective and vision, your skills and strengths and all of the things that make you who you are.

bring
your
own
sunshine

Wherever you go, bring your own sunshine.
Spread love and light. Radiate positivity.
Inspire the world with your smile.

Focus on the good

Focus on doing what's good for you and putting good into the world.

CHIN UP

Be brave. Keep your chin up and always do the best you can.

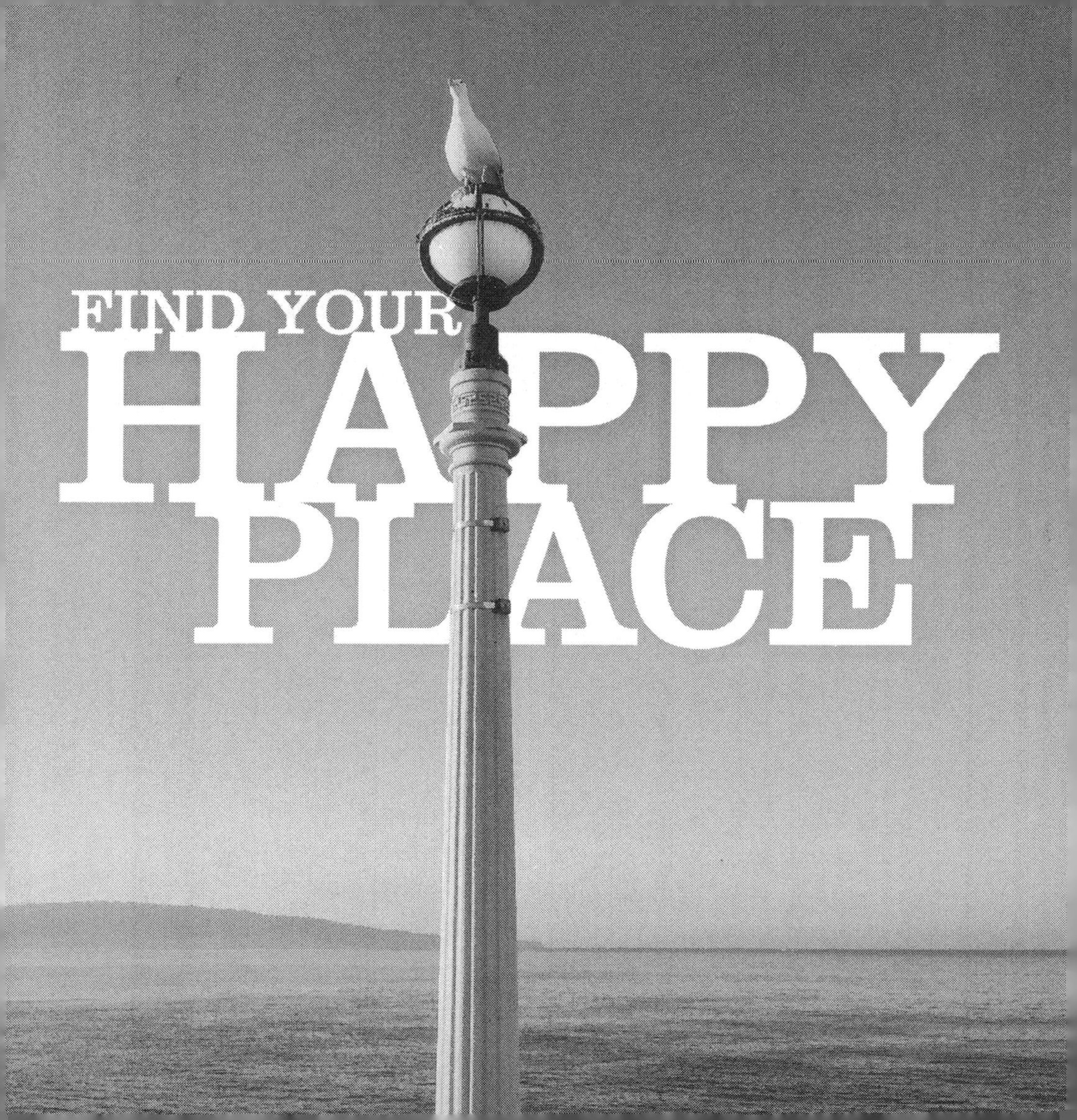
FIND YOUR
HAPPY
PLACE

Think about the people, activities and places that make you happy...spend time with those people, do more of those things, explore those places...do more of what makes you happy.

GET
LOST

Sometimes you have to get lost in order to find your true self. Go out and discover your world and devote yourself to it with all your heart.

THERE ARE
BLESSINGS
IN EVERY DAY

While it may not always seem like it, and not every day is amazing and perfect…there are blessings in every day.

Remember to look for them. Be open to them. And be grateful for every blessing.

STOP AND LOOK AROUND

Life moves fast.
Don't miss it.

BE FREAKIN'
AWESOME

In my book, being awesome means being passionate, living a life you love, inspiring others to be better than they were yesterday, and being honorable...

Whatever your definition is...just be awesome!

ENJOY LIFE

You only get one life. Enjoy it!

HAPPINESS IS A CHOICE

Are you choosing to be happy today?

Explore. Do something new. Go on an adventure.

know
your
worth

Remember to not only value yourself more, but also strive to become more valuable, and both happiness and success will follow.

YOU CAN
HANDLE
ANYTHING
THAT THIS
WEEK THROWS
AT YOU.

With so many accessible resources, support from friends and family, and your own strength and resilience…you can handle anything.

YOU ARE

WHO

YOU ARE

You are a unique and beautiful human being.
Embrace your qualities.
Love who you are.

YOU
ARE CAPABLE OF
AMAZING
THINGS

There will be doubters and haters. There will be obstacles and setbacks. There will be mistakes and failures. Don't let anything keep you from accomplishing great things.

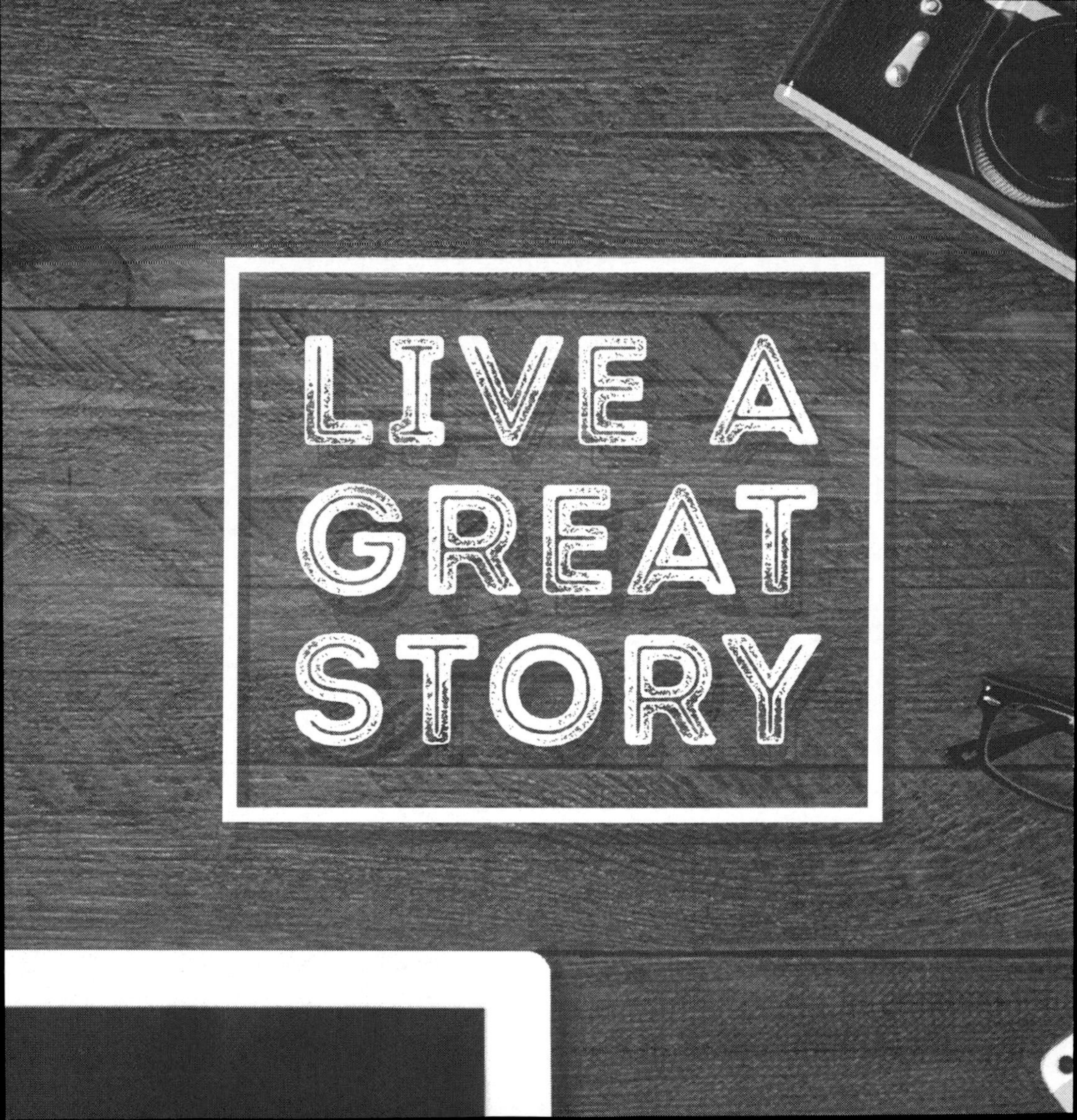
LIVE A
GREAT
STORY

Remember to do what you love.
Do what makes you happy.
Create some amazing memories.
Live a great story.

DO WHAT YOU LOVE

Do the things that truly make you happy.

do your own thing

Do your own thing and don't worry about what others think of you...

HAPPINESS
REQUIRES
EFFORT

I often need to be reminded that happiness is a choice and often requires effort. Remember to leave behind anything that doesn't bring you joy and consciously focus on being grateful, hopeful and positive.

MAKE
SOMEONE
SMILE
TODAY

Happiness is touching someone's heart
and making someone smile.

MAKE
YOURSELF
PROUD

Live a life you are proud of.

BE KNOWN FOR YOUR
KINDNESS
&
GRACE

A little bit of kindness and grace go a long way.

BE
AWESOME
★ TODAY ★

Be productive. Be positive. Be grateful. Be happy.
Be kind. Be freakin' awesome today!

Spread the love. Pay it forward. Be a blessing.

pay
it
forward

Be kind to everyone you meet. Lend a helping hand, share your smile and give freely to the world your gift of love.

do good

good

feel good

Be good. Do good. Feel good.

WALK A MILE IN THEIR SHOES

Have more empathy and respect toward others. There's no room for bullying, harassment, hatred, exploitation and intolerance. No one should have the right to take someone else's happiness away.

PROGRESS
NOT
PERFECTION

Do your best while not stressing about making everything perfect. Be productive and just make progress.

Inspire people to live passionately and find
the good in every day.

dream it
then do it

Stay motivated.

Stay hungry.

Stay focused.

Pursue your dream and make it a reality.

EVERYONE BENEFITS FROM YOUR HAPPINESS

Remember to spread happiness and radiate positivity.

BEAUTY

Thank you for making the world a better and more beautiful place.

Make someone smile today.
And pursue whatever makes your heart smile.

GRATITUDE
IS A STATE OF BEING

Remember to choose to be grateful.
Make it a habit to appreciate life's gifts.
Embody gratitude.
Express gratitude.
Cultivate gratitude.

be a

LIGHT

to everyone you meet

Everyone is going through something.
We all struggle. We all have our own battles
and demons to fight.

Be kind to everyone you meet. A kind word.
A helping hand. They make a difference. One small
gesture may turn around someone's day or change
a life for the better.

be happy

Do what makes you happy.

FUTURE
DREAM
SELF

What are you dreaming of doing or being? Envision what you want for your life and start becoming your future dream self.

laugh at
yourself

Remember to not take life too seriously. Laughter can be a powerful weapon against negativity. Sometimes you just have to laugh at yourself.

celebrate GOOD times

Remember that not every day will be wonderful. Some days you have to create your own sunshine. Find something you are grateful for and celebrate the good times.

TAKE CARE
of
EACH
OTHER

Everyone benefits from your happiness and kindness.
Spread love wherever you go.

REFRESH

Remember to take the time to refresh your spirit.
Reinvigorate your soul. Restore your mind.
And revitalize your body.

be good to people

Be good to people.
Be good people.

Just love.

SIMPLY BE
HAPPIER

Remember to simply be happier. Happiness is a choice. Do what makes you happy.

Be fearless. Be daring. Seek new experiences and jump into new opportunities. Get out of your comfort zone. Be rad!

inspire

All I want is to inspire you to be the best version of yourself. And to follow your passions, pursue your dreams and unlock your full potential. And to come alive by doing what you love and what makes you happy.

wake up *and* LIVE

Live a life full of wonder, gratitude and positivity.
Do what makes you happy.

your {uniqueness} *is your magic*

Remember that there are 7 billion people on this planet and only one YOU. The world needs your magic.

Spread love.
Spread laughter.
Spread positivity.
Spread happiness.

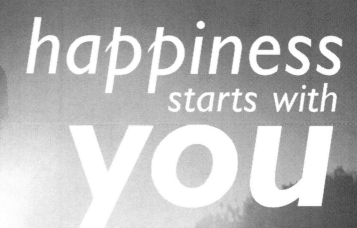

It all starts with you.
Do what you love.
Do what makes you happy.

GO FIND
your best
SELF

Remember to work on your weaknesses while engaging your strengths. Improve your skills and identify your talents. Discover your passions and visualize what you want your life to be. Strive to be better than you were yesterday.

CREATE

a life worth living

Remember to create a life that you love.
Make choices that give you a sense of pride and help
you grow. Move on from anything that doesn't bring
you joy. Do what makes you happy.

GIVE
IT ALL YOU HAVE
WHILE YOU STILL
CAN

Do what you can,
With what you have,
Where you are.

If you aren't chasing your dreams now…when?
If you aren't creating a life you love now…when?
If you aren't taking care of your health now…when?

LIFE *is a* GIFT

Life is a gift. Don't take it for granted.

Do something memorable.
Go on an adventure.
Do what makes you happy.

INVEST
in
YOURSELF

The most important place you can put your time and money is YOURSELF.

SHINE

in your own way

It's your time to shine. Shine in your own way.

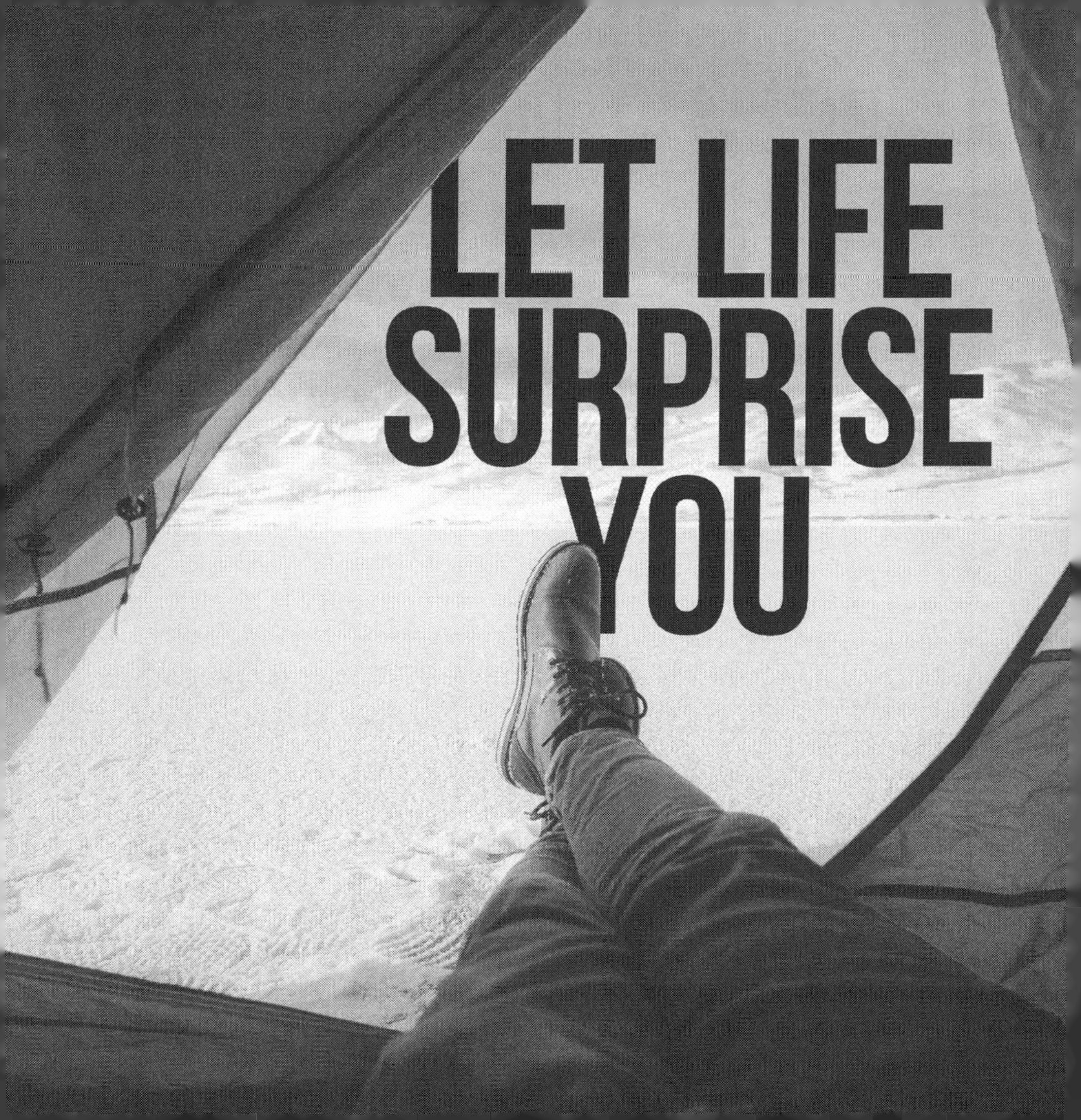
LET LIFE
SURPRISE
YOU

Let go and allow life the freedom to amaze you.

LIVE *your* DREAM

Dream big and passionately pursue your dream!

Be who you want to be.
Create the life you want to live.
Be YOU.

RISE

BY LIFTING OTHERS

The higher you lift the people around you...the higher you rise.

THRIVE

don't just survive

Life is too short to be complacent or just go through
the motions. Do something different every day.
Something that fuels your passions. Something that
gets you closer to your dream. Do your best.
Feel your best. Thrive.

Happiness is often magnified when it's shared.
Seek new experiences and make life an adventure.
Create memories that remain with you forever.

TIME
is precious

Time is precious. Spend it doing what makes you happy
and spend it with someone who makes you happy.

EAT
SLEEP
LIVE WELL

Eat healthy. Rest physically and mentally. Live in a way that allows you to be at peace with your life.

It's scary how fast time flies. Don't let life pass you by. Be grateful for each moment. Savor every bite. Appreciate life now.

peace
+
harmony

Violence resolves nothing. Respect each other in spite of our differences. Help bring harmony to our world by cultivating love and peace for all.

YOUR LIFE
IS YOUR MESSAGE
SO MAKE SURE IT'S
INSPIRING

What do you want your legacy to be? What do you want to be known for? You get this one life…make it memorable. Make it amazing. Make it inspiring.

★ WITH **vigor**

Do what makes you happy and what makes you feel alive. Flourish. Make good choices. Be healthy. Do everything with vigor.

live life out LOUD

Remember to be bold. Be brave. Let your creativity be seen and your voice be heard. Live life out loud.

CULTIVATE LOVE

In response to the senseless violence.
The disrespect and intolerance.
The hatred and negativity.

Let's cultivate some LOVE today.

{ CRAFT YOUR }

LEGACY

What do you want to be known for?
How do you want to be remembered?
What do you want your legacy to be?

GIVE
IT
YOUR
ALL

Give it everything you have while you still can.
No regrets.

say yes to new ADVENTURES

Say yes to new experiences, meeting new people and exploring new places. Say yes to making life one big adventure.

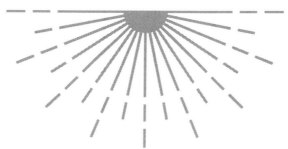

Good health is such a vital key to happiness. Take care of your body and mind. Eat right. Exercise. Do your best to feel your best, because health is wealth.

GRAT·I·TUDE

noun [grat-i-tood, -tyood]

the quality of being thankful; readiness to show
appreciation for and to return kindness:

Remember to be thankful.
Appreciate kindness and return kindness.

FIND SOMETHING THAT MAKES YOU HAPPY AND USE IT TO MAKE OTHERS HAPPY

Remember to do what makes you happy and pursue your passion. Find something that makes you come alive and make that your purpose. Inspire others to do the same.

LET
YOUR
OWN
LIGHT
SHINE

Radiate positivity and spread happiness.

Remember to focus on what moves and excites you.
Do what you love. Love what you do.
Live passionately.

Love is universal.

DO a kind deed.

SPEAK a kind word.

THINK a kind thought.

Practice kindness.
Always.

LET PEACE BE YOUR PATH

We need more compassion,
more tolerance,
more respect
and more love in this world.
There is way too much hate.
Let peace be your path.

MAKE
YOUR
MARK

Do something significant, that will impact the lives
of many and change the world for the better.
Make your mark!

CHANGE
THE
WORLD

I am on a mission to inspire passion, purpose and positivity. To help people live happier and healthier lives. To remind people to live with gratitude and spread love. To empower people to reach their full potential.

Join my tribe...this movement...and we will change the world together!

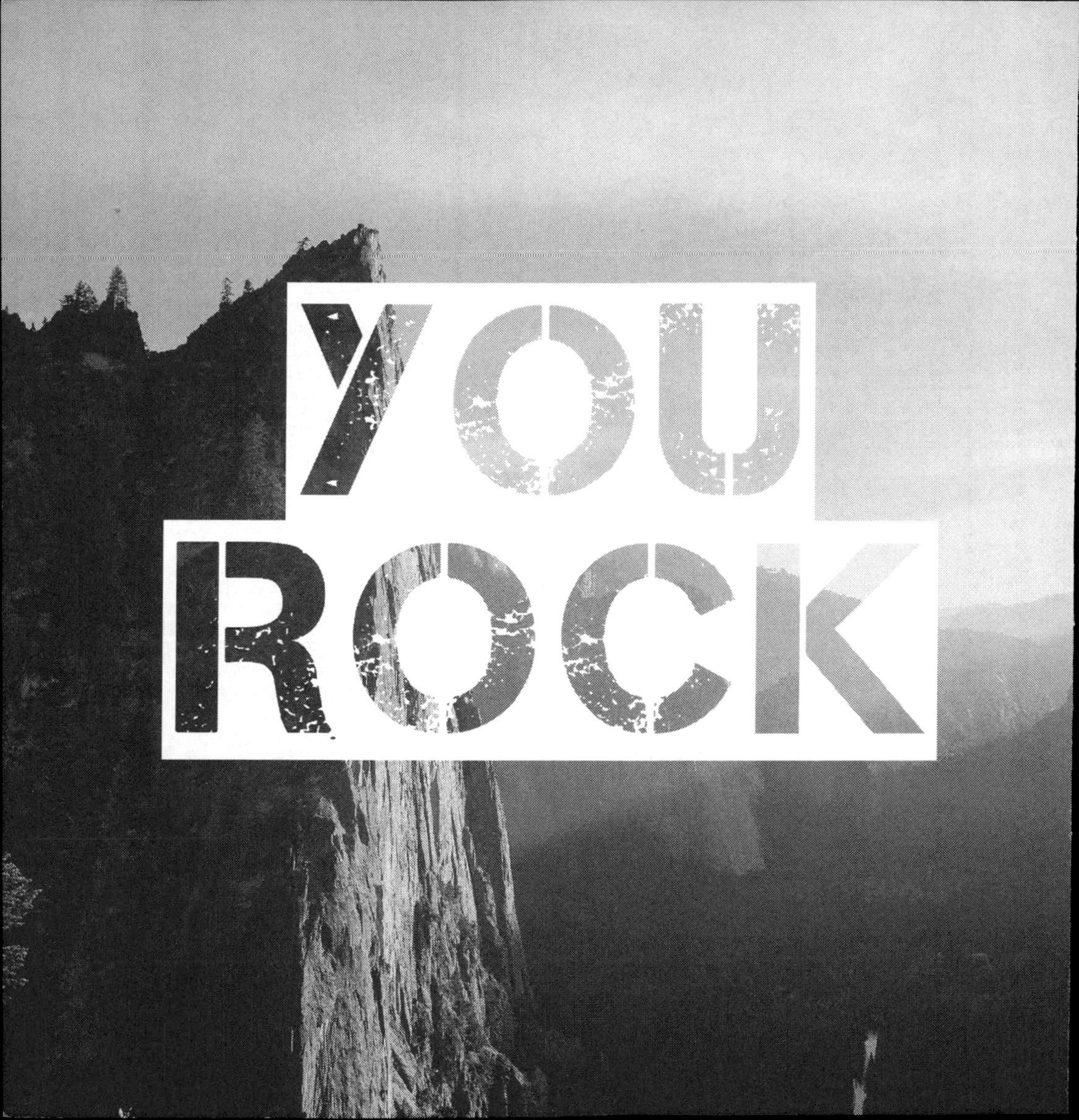
YOU
ROCK

Just wanted to take a second to say THANK YOU for reading this and supporting me and The Happy Project! Your support fuels my creativity every day. Keep pursuing your passion and spreading positivity, love and light. You make this world a better place.

I would love to hear any feedback you have. Or drop me a note and tell me which image resonated most with you. You can find me on Instagram, Pinterest, Tumblr, Linkedin, Facebook and of course on TheHappyProject.com.

Photo by Marilyn Nakazato

Photo by Emil Fernandez

ABOUT THE AUTHOR

Lance Kitagawa is a designer who is passionate about creating beautiful things to inspire people and change the world. He lives in Los Angeles. Please join his tribe at TheHappyProject.com.

ACKNOWLEDGEMENTS

Thank you to my editors, May Kitagawa and Jared Barris, for thoroughly scrutinizing my work and helping me make this book that much better.
Photographs primarily from Unsplash.com and a few from Death To Stock Photo, Gratisography, Jay Mantri, Moveast, and Life of Pix. Font on back cover is Butler. (www.creativecommons.org/licenses/by-sa/4.0 legalcode)

THANK YOU

To all of my fans, family and friends who have given me the opportunity to come alive by doing what I love...thank you for your part in my journey.

Made in the USA
Lexington, KY
26 September 2017